FRETBOARD ROADMAPS 5-STRING BANJO

THE ESSENTIAL PATTERNS THAT ALL THE PROS KNOW AND USE

BY FRED SOKOLOW

PLAYBACK+

Speed • Pitch • Balance • Loop

To access audio visit:
www.halleonard.com/mylibrary

7158-4118-8389-0968

RECORDING CREDITS
Banjo, Guitar, Mandolin and Vocals—Fred Sokolow
Sound Engineer and Other Instruments—Dennis O'Hanlon
Recorded at O'Hanlon Recording and Music Services

ISBN 978-0-634-00143-7

HAL•LEONARD®

7777 W. BLUEMOUND RD. P.O. BOX 13819 MILWAUKEE, WI 53213

Visit Hal Leonard Online at
www.halleonard.com

CONTENTS

SONG INDEX

INTRODUCTION

Accomplished banjo players can *ad lib* hot solos and play backup in any key—all over the fretboard. They know several different soloing approaches and can choose the style that fits the tune, whether it's a folk or country tune, hard driving bluegrass, Dixieland or jazz.

There are moveable patterns on the banjo fretboard that make it easy to do these things. The pros are aware of these "fretboard roadmaps," even if they don't read music. If you want to jam with other players, *this is essential banjo knowledge.*

You need the fretboard roadmaps if...

▶ All your soloing sounds the same and you want some different styles and flavors from which to choose.

▶ You don't know how to play in every key.

▶ Your banjo fretboard beyond the 5th fret is mysterious, uncharted territory.

▶ You can't automatically play any familiar melody.

▶ You know a lot of "bits and pieces" on the banjo, but you don't have a system that ties it all together.

Read on, and many mysteries will be explained. The pages that follow can shed light and save you a great deal of time.

Good luck,

Fred Sokolow

THE RECORDING AND THE PRACTICE TRACKS

All the licks, riffs and tunes in this book are played on the accompanying recording. There are also five *Practice Tracks* on the recording. They are mixed so that the banjo is on one side of your stereo and the backup band is on the other.

Each track illustrates one or more **ROADMAP** concepts, such as melodic soloing, or moveable chord-based licks. You can also tune out the banjo track and use the backup tracks to practice playing solos.

PRELIMINARIES

TUNING

This book teaches 5-string in *open G tuning*, because it's by far the most widespread tuning currently in use. Old time banjo players (who play traditional, pre-bluegrass, mountain music) use many tunings, including G, D, C, Double-C and G modal; bluegrass pickers *occasionally* use them. They're wonderful for specific tunes, but the open G is more versatile.

Use a tuning device or the string-to-string method described below to tune the banjo to an open (unfretted) G chord:

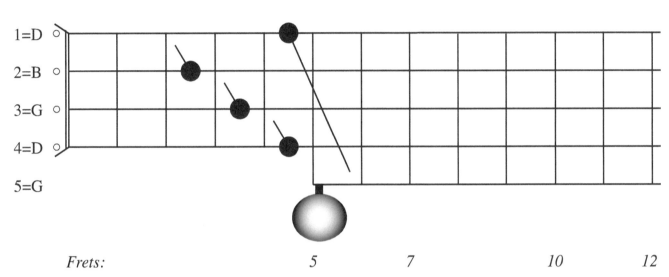

As the above diagram shows, once you've tuned the open 4th/D string, you can:

▶ Tune the 3rd string/G by matching it to the 4th string/5th fret,

▶ Tune the 2nd string/B by matching it to the 3rd string/4th fret,

▶ Tune the 1st string/D by matching it to the 2nd string/3rd fret,

▶ Tune the 5th string/G by matching it to the 1st string/5th fret.

PICKING PATTERNS

There are a lot of ways to pick and strum the banjo. Bluegrassers use the thumb, index and middle fingers, wearing picks, and call it three-finger picking. Traditional or old-time mountain music players do a strum that's called *clawhammer* or *frailing*. Dixieland or jazz banjo players strum with a flatpick, avoiding the 5th string, although the four-string banjo is used more commonly to play these styles.

► CLAWHAMMER/FRAILING

They call it *clawhammer* because your picking hand takes on a claw-like shape when you play this bump-ditty, rolling rhythm:

1. Pick down on a single string, such as the 1st string, with the fingernail of your index or middle finger.

2. Brush down on the 3rd, 2nd and 1st strings with the same finger you used for Step 1.

3. Pick the 5th string with your thumb.

Try this over and over, and play along with the recording.

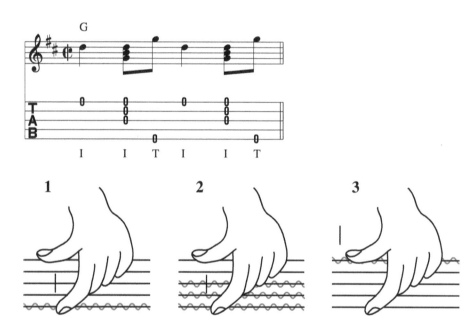

► THE BASIC STRUM

Many folk banjo players do a variation of the clawhammer style in which Step 1 is an index finger up-pick instead of a down pick. This "basic strum" is exactly the same as clawhammer style, except the single note of Step 1 is not played with the fingernail, so it has a less percussive sound. Some people find it easier than clawhammer picking.

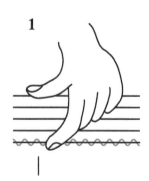

▶ A WALTZ (3/4 TIME) STRUM

Here's a 3/4 time variation of the basic strum:

1. Pick *up* on a single string, such as the 1st string, with your index finger.

2. Brush down on the 3rd, 2nd and 1st strings with the fingernail of your middle or ring finger.

3. Pick the 5th string with your thumb.

4. Repeat Steps 2 and 3

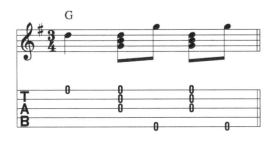

▶ THREE-FINGER PICKING

Often called "Scruggs style," after the great banjo innovator, Earl Scruggs, this style is based on thumb-and-two-finger patterns, like these:

Forward Roll

I M T I M T I M

In and Out Roll

T I T M T I T M

Forward-Backward

T I M T M I T M

Tag-Ending Roll

I M T I M I T M

Foggy Mountain Breakdown Roll

I M I M T I M T

The last one gets its name from the famous Scruggs instrumental. Play each roll over and over until you gain some speed.

► **DIXIELAND STRUMMING**

Play this rhythm, which is mostly downstrokes with the flatpick:

⊓ = Downstroke
∨ = Upstroke

FIRST POSITION CHORDS

Here are some simple, basic chords. The numbers indicate fingering:

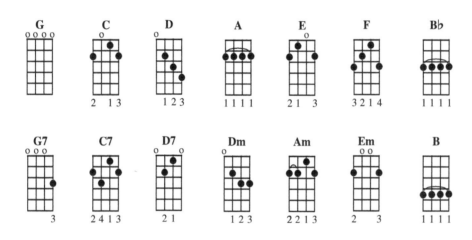

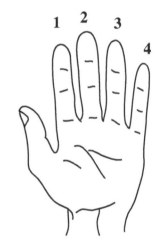

PUTTING IT ALL TOGETHER

The following tunes will give you a chance to practice chord changes and the above strums and picking patterns. Listen to each song before you start playing. Play each one as slowly as you need to, in order to keep the rhythm smooth and steady. As soon as you can, play along with the recording.

 # Worried Man Blues (Clawhammer)

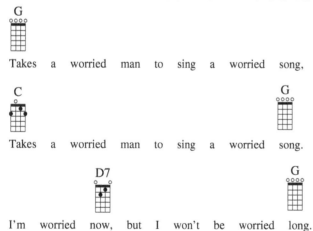

Red River Valley (In-and-Out Roll)

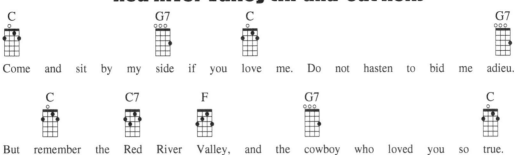

C					G7				C										G7

Come and sit by my side if you love me. Do not hasten to bid me adieu.

C		C7		F			G7					C

But remember the Red River Valley, and the cowboy who loved you so true.

Wreck of Old 97 (Foggy Mountain Breakdown Roll)

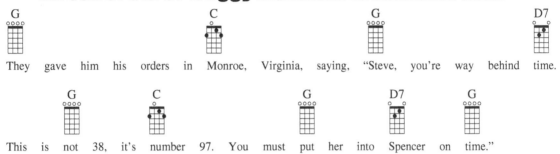

G						C					G				D7

They gave him his orders in Monroe, Virginia, saying, "Steve, you're way behind time.

G				C				G			D7		G

This is not 38, it's number 97. You must put her into Spencer on time."

Amazing Grace (3/4 Time Strum)

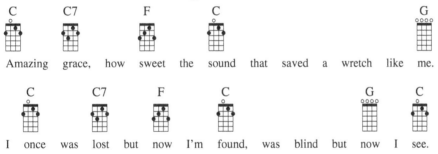

C	C7		F		C						G

Amazing grace, how sweet the sound that saved a wretch like me.

C		C7		F		C				G	C

I once was lost but now I'm found, was blind but now I see.

Gambler's Blues (Dixieland Strum)

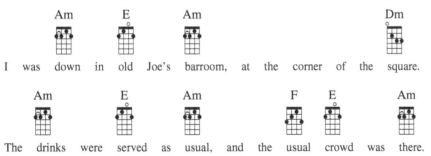

Am		E		Am						Dm

I was down in old Joe's barroom, at the corner of the square.

Am		E		Am				F	E		Am

The drinks were served as usual, and the usual crowd was there.

NOTES ON THE FRETBOARD

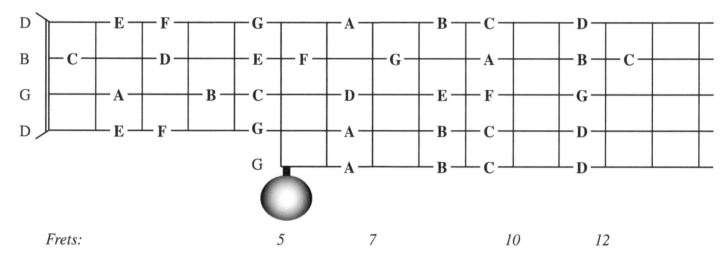

Frets: 5 7 10 12

WHY?

▶ Knowing where the notes are will help you find chords and scales up and down the neck. It will help you alter and understand chords (e.g., *How do I flat the seventh in this chord? Why is this chord minor instead of major?*). It's a first step toward understanding music.

WHAT?

▶ *The notes get higher in pitch as you go up the alphabet and up the fretboard.*

▶ *A whole step is two frets, and a half step is one fret.*

▶ *Sharps are one fret higher:* 1st string/3rd fret = F, so 1st string/4th fret = F♯.

▶ *Flats are one fret lower:* 3rd string/2nd fret = A, so 3rd string/1st fret = A♭.

HOW?

▶ *The banjo is tuned G–D–G–B–D* (from 5th to 1st string). **Start by learning these notes!**

▶ *Fretboard markings help.* Most banjos have fretboard inlays or marks on the neck indicating the 5th, 7th, 10th and 12th frets. Become aware of these signposts.

▶ *The 5th and 1st string notes are the same,* once you get past the 5th fret.

▶ *The 4th and 1st string notes are the same,* but an octave apart.

DO IT!

▶ *Learn other notes in reference to the notes you already know.*

▷ *The notes at the 2nd fret are a whole step* (or one step of the alphabet) *higher than the "open-string" (unfretted) notes.* The open 4th string/2nd fret = D, so 4th string/2nd fret = E.

▷ *Everything starts over at the 12 fret.* The open 1st string is D, so the 1st string/12th fret is also D.

▷ *You already know some notes from the string-to-string tuning method* (in the PRELIMINARIES chapter: the 3rd string/4th fret = B, 2nd string/3rd fret = D, and so on).

SUMMING UP — NOW YOU KNOW...

▶ *The location of the notes on the fretboard*

▶ *The meaning of these musical terms:*

Whole Step

Half Step

Sharp (♯)

Flat (♭)

THE MAJOR SCALE

C Major Scale

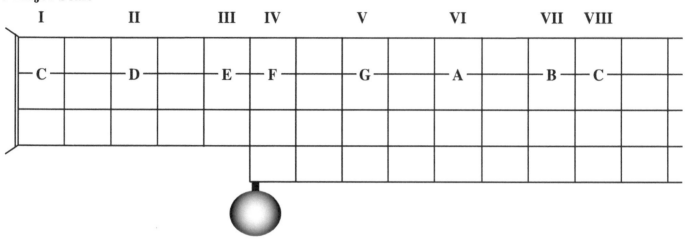

WHY?

▶ To understand music and to communicate with other players, you need to know about the major scale. The major scale is a ruler that helps you measure distances between notes and chords. Knowing the major scale will help you understand and talk about chord construction, scales and chord relationships.

WHAT?

▶ *The major scale is the "Do–Re–Mi" scale you have heard all your life.* Countless familiar tunes are composed of notes from this scale.

▶ *Intervals are distances between notes.* The intervals of the major scale are used to describe these distances. For example, E is the third note of the C major scale, and it is four frets above C (see above). This distance is called a *third*. Similarly, A is a third above F, and C♯ is a third above A. On the banjo, *a third is always a distance of four frets.*

HOW?

▶ *Every major scale has the same interval pattern of whole and half-steps:*

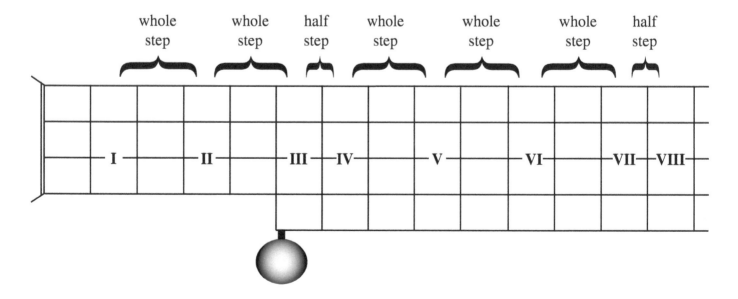

In other words, the major scale ascends by whole steps (two frets at a time) with two exceptions: there is a half step (one fret) from the third to the fourth notes and from the seventh to the eighth notes. It's helpful to think of intervals in terms of frets (e.g., a third is 4 frets).

▶ *Intervals can extend above the octave.* They correspond to lower intervals:

same as I		same as II			same as IV				same as VI	
VII—VIII		IX		XI				XIII		

DO IT!

▶ *Learn the major scale intervals* by playing any note and finding the note that is a third higher, a fourth and fifth higher, etc.

SUMMING UP — NOW YOU KNOW...

▶ *The intervals of the major scale and the number of frets that make up each interval .*

FIRST POSITION MAJOR SCALES

C Major Scale

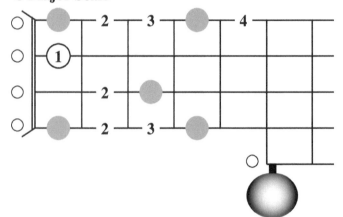

G Major Scale

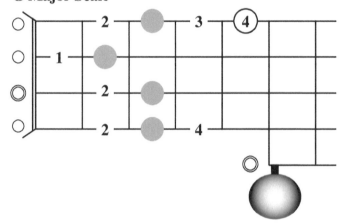

D Major Scale

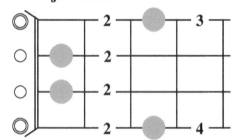

E Major Scale

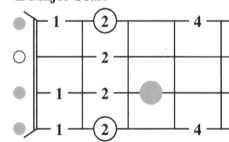

F Major Scale

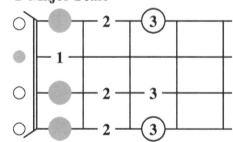

WHY?

▶ Whether they're playing a hot fiddle tune, picking the melody to a ballad or improvising a solo, banjo players often use first position major scales. Familiarity with these scales helps in all these areas. (Most 5-string players use a capo to play in keys other than those diagrammed in **ROADMAP #3.**)

WHAT?

▶ *Every key has its own scale and characteristic licks.* You use the C scale to play in the key of C, the E scale to play in E, and so on.

▶ *Each scale (and the licks that go with it) can be played throughout a tune,* in spite of chord changes within the tune.

▶ *A root is the note that gives the scale its name.*

▶ *The root notes in each scale are circled.* The numbers are suggested fingerings.

▶ *The grey circles are "blue notes,"* flatted 3rds, 5ths and 7ths. They add a bluesy flavor to the scales.

HOW?

▶ *Put your hand "in position" for each scale by fingering the appropriate chord* (e.g., play a C chord to get in position for the C major scale). You don't have to maintain the chord while playing the scale, but it's a reference point (see page 8).

► *Play "up and down" each of the following scales until it feels comfortable and familiar.*
Play the chord before playing the scale, and "loop" the scale—play it several times in a
row, with no pause between repetitions:

C Major Scale

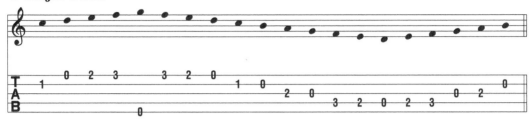

G Major Scale

D Major Scale

E Major Scale

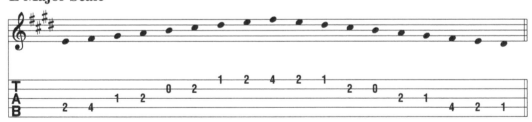

F Major Scale

DO IT!

▶ The following solos show how to use all five major scales to play melodies. They are different versions of "Worried Man Blues." Some are played clawhammer style, some bluegrass style. In either style, you pick the melody and "fill in" the spaces between melody notes with rolls or strums (steps 2 and 3 of the clawhammer strum). In both styles, play the appropriate chord changes when they occur.

The first version of "Worried Man Blues" is played clawhammer style. All the melody notes come from the C major scale, with a few blue notes thrown in.

Worried Man Blues — C

The key-of-G version of "Worried Man Blues" makes use of the "Foggy Mountain Breakdown" roll. When there's a pause between melody notes, the rolls fill the gap and keep the rhythm going.

Worried Man Blues — G

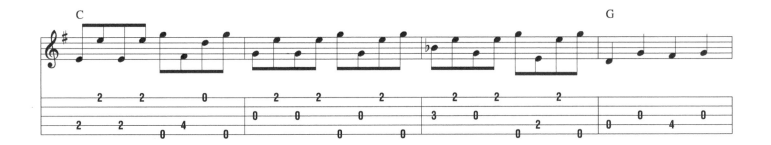

Here's a key-of-D clawhammer version of "Worried Man Blues." When playing in D, tune the 5th string two frets higher than usual, to A. This works because there's an A note in a D chord. Match the 5th string to the 1st string/7th fret.

Worried Man Blues — D

This key-of-E version of the tune consists mostly of forward rolls. It's an improvisation, rather than the song's melody. When playing in E, tune the 5th string to B (match it to the 1st string/9th fret) or to G♯ (match it to the 1st string/6th fret).

15 **Worried Man Blues — E**

This clawhammer version of "Worried Man Blues" is a major-scale-based improvisation, with blue notes added into the mix. When playing in F, tune the 5th string up to A (match it to the 1st string/7th fret).

16 **Worried Man Blues — F**

SUMMING UP — NOW YOU KNOW...

▶ *How to play five first-position major scales (C, G, D, F and E) and how to use them to play licks and solos*

▶ *The meaning of the musical term "blue notes," and how to add them to major scales and melodies*

▶ *How to use major scales to play a melody, clawhammer style and bluegrass style*

▶ *How to re-tune the 5th string to play in the keys of D, F and E*

4

THREE MOVEABLE MAJOR CHORDS AND THEIR VARIATIONS

Barre

D Formation

F Formation

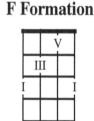

WHY?

► **ROADMAP #4** will help you build a full chord vocabulary. Some chords require the use of barred or moveable positions, and this chapter shows how to play almost any chord you need.

WHAT?

► A **chord** is a group of three or more notes played simultaneously.

► A **moveable chord** can be played all over the fretboard. It contains no open (unfretted) strings.

► A **root** is the note that gives a chord its name.

► *The three moveable major chords of* **ROADMAP #4** *(and all major chords) consist of roots, 3rds and 5ths.* Make sure you know the intervals in these three formations (e.g., the 4th and 1st strings in the D formation are 3rds).

► *You can play dozens of chords (minors, sevenths, major sevenths, etc.) by altering slightly the three basic, moveable major chords of* **ROADMAP #4.** For example, you can play one fret lower on one string to make a major chord minor. This is an easy way to expand your chord vocabulary.

HOW?

► *The 3rd string is the root of the barred chord formation.* It's a C chord when played at the 5th fret, because the 3rd string/5th fret is C. At the 7th fret it's a D chord, and so on.

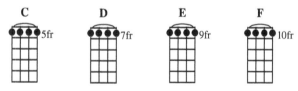

► *The 2nd string is the root of the D formation.* When you play the D formation at the 4th fret, the 2nd string is at the 5th fret, so it's an E chord.

E   4fr   F   5fr   G   7fr   A   9fr

► *The 4th and 1st strings are roots of the F formation.* When you play the F formation at the 3rd fret, the 1st and 4th strings are at the 5th fret, so it's a G chord.

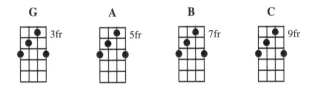

► *There are four types of chords:*

▷ *Major chords* consist of a root (1), 3rd and 5th.

▷ *Minor chords* consist of a root, flatted 3rd and 5th.

▷ *Seventh chords* consist of a root, 3rd, 5th and flatted 7th.

▷ *Diminished chords* consist of a root, flatted 3rd, flatted 5th, and double-flatted 7th (which is the same as a 6th).

► *All other chords are variations of these four types.* For example:

▷ C6 is a C major chord with a 6th added (1, 3, 5, 6).

▷ Gm7 is a G minor chord with a flatted seventh (1, ♭3, 5, ♭7).

DO IT!

► *Play the three moveable formations (F formation, D formation, barre), all over the fretboard and name them.*

► *Compare every new chord you learn to a basic chord you already know.* Every small chord grid in the "DO IT" section, below, is a variation of a basic chord formation.

► *Here are the most-played chords.* Play them and compare each formation to the larger grid to the left, from which it is derived.

Barre

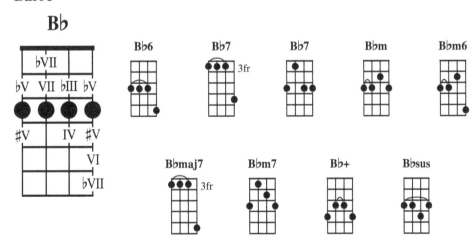

D Formation

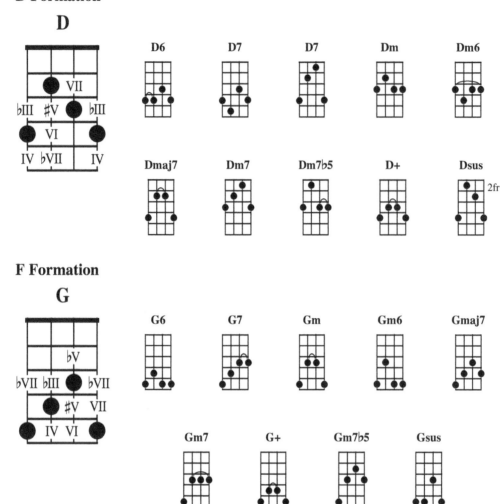

F Formation

DIMINISHED

▶ The diminished chord (1, ♭3, ♭5, ♭♭7) repeats every 3 frets. The following are all A diminished chords:

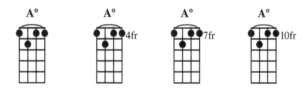

▶ A diminished chord can be named by any of its four notes. For example, an A° can also be called C°, E♭° or F♯°, depending on the context in which it occurs.

SUMMING UP — NOW YOU KNOW...

▶ *How to play any major chord three ways:* Using a barre, D or F formation

▶ *The formulas for major, minor, 7th and diminished chords,* and how to play them using moveable formations

▶ *How to vary the moveable major chords* to play many chord types: minors, sevenths, sixths, etc.

▶ *The meaning of these musical terms:*

Chord, Moveable Chord, Root

THE F-D-BARRE ROADMAP

F Chords

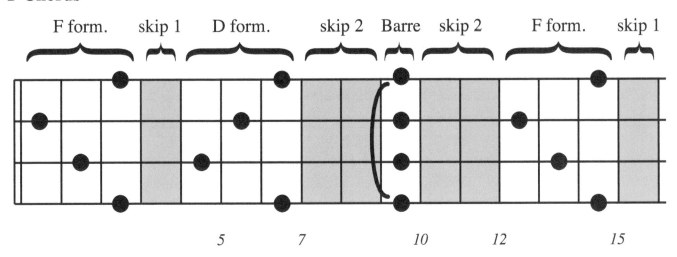

F form.   skip 1   D form.   skip 2   Barre   skip 2   F form.   skip 1

5   7   10   12   15

WHY?

▶ The **"F-D-BARRE" ROADMAP** shows you how to play any major chord all over the fretboard, using the three major chord formations of **ROADMAP #4.** It's useful for locating chords up and down the neck, and for finding a higher voicing of a chord.

WHAT?

▶ The chords in the fretboard diagram above are all F chords.

HOW?

▶ *To memorize this roadmap,* remember: *F-SKIP 1, D-SKIP 2, Barre-SKIP 2.* In other words, play an F formation, skip a fret; play a D formation, skip two frets; play a barre formation, skip two frets.

▶ Use the F-D-Barre roadmap to play all the D chords:

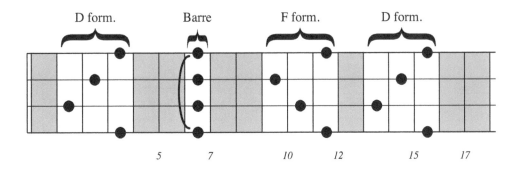

D form.   Barre   F form.   D form.

5   7   10   12   15   17

▶ Notice that you can climb the fretboard *starting with any chord formation.* The F-D-Barre roadmap is a continuous loop that you can enter at any point. It can be the D-Barre-F or Barre-F-D roadmap. The "skips" are always the same: one skip after F, two after D, two after the barre.

▶ You can add notes (6ths, 7ths, major 7ths, etc.) to the F, D and Barre formations to create countless licks, as shown in **ROADMAP #4.**

DO IT!

> ▶ *Play the following backup to the old folk song, "Sloop John B."* The tune lingers for several bars on each chord, giving you the opportunity to play several formations for every D, G and Barre chord.

Sloop John B.

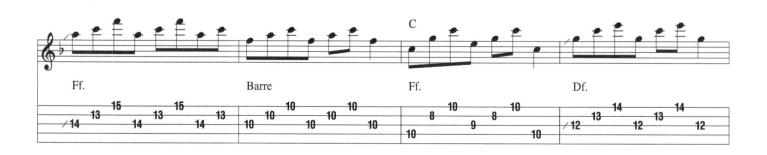

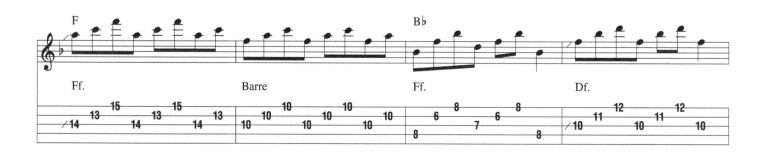

▶ *Use the F-D-Barre chords to play a solo to the country standard, "Wabash Cannonball."* This solo consists of ascending and descending chord formations, with many chord variations (6ths, 7ths, etc.).

Wabash Cannonball

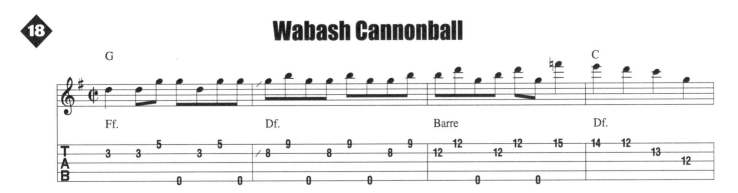

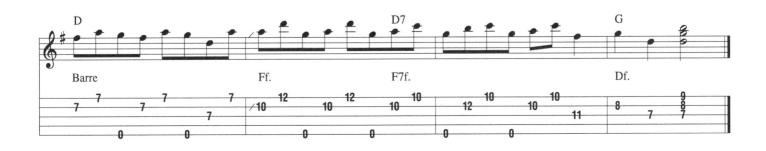

Here's another solo based on the F-D-Barre chords. "Great Speckled Bird," popularized by Roy Acuff, has the same melody as "I'm Thinking Tonight of My Blue Eyes," "The Prisoner's Song," "Wild Side of Life," and many other country/bluegrass standards. In this clawhammer arrangement, you often jump to a higher inversion of a chord in order to find melody notes. (Tune your 5th string to A. Match it to the 1st string/7th fret.)

Great Speckled Bird

SUMMING UP — NOW YOU KNOW...

► *How to play three major chord fragments*

► *How to use them to play any major chord all over the fretboard* (with the F-D-Barre roadmap)

► *How to vary them with 6ths, 7ths, etc., to create countless licks*

#6 CHORD FRAGMENT/CHORD FAMILIES

Three G Chord Families:

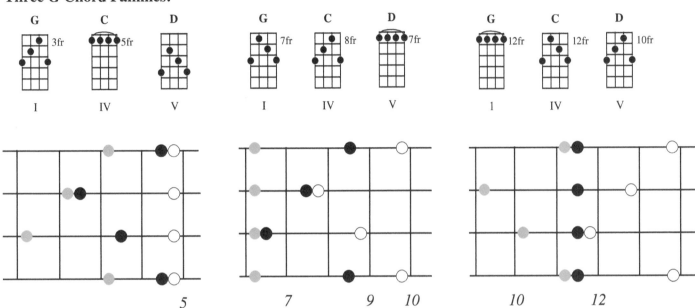

- ● = I Chord
- ○ = IV Chord
- ◐ = V Chord

WHY?

▶ It's easier to learn new tunes and create solos when you understand "chord families" and know how to play them all over the fretboard. **ROADMAP #6** arranges the three moveable major chords of **ROADMAP #5** into chord families.

WHAT?

▶ *Every song has a chord progression,* a repeated chord sequence in which each chord is played for a certain number of bars.

▶ *Thousands of tunes consist of just three chords: the I, IV and V chords. These three chords are a "chord family."* "I," "IV" and "V" refer to steps of the major scale of your key.

▷ The I chord is the key. In the key of C, C is the I chord, because C is the first note in the C major scale.

▷ The IV chord is the chord whose root is the fourth note in the major scale of your key. In the key of C, F is the IV chord, since F is the fourth note in the C major scale.

▷ The V chord is the chord whose root is the fifth note in the major scale of your key. In the key of C, G is the V chord, since G is the fifth note in the C scale.

▶ **ROADMAP #6** *shows three ways of playing the "key of G" chord family:* with an F formation/I chord, a D formation/I chord, and a barred/I chord.

► *The relationships in* **ROADMAP #6** *are moveable. Once you learn them, you can make chord changes automatically.* For example, in any key, if you're playing a I chord with an F formation, the V chord is the D formation a fret lower.

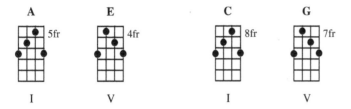

DO IT!

► *This solo to a standard I–IV–V progression will give you some practice memorizing the chord family relationships.*

Island Fragments

► *Here's a similar exercise, but with a I–V–IV–I progression.* Using **ROADMAP #6**, you could easily play the same solo in any key.

It's All in the Family

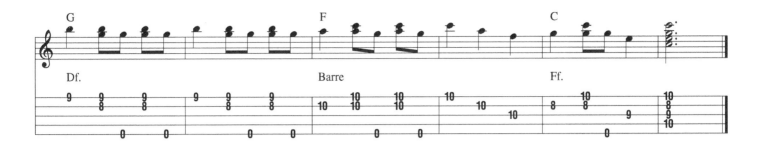

▶ *Countless bluegrass standards have a I–IV–I–V progression similar to "Wreck of Old 97." The ad lib, clawhammer solo that follows makes use of two moveable, key-of-G chord families, and includes hammer-ons and pull-offs.*

▷ To play a hammer-on, sound a note by fretting a string suddenly with your fretting finger (rather than picking it with your picking hand).

▷ To play a pull-off, sound a note by plucking downward on a string with your fretting finger.

Wreck of Old 97 (With Moveable Chords)

► *Many bluegrass, country, folk and swing standards are based on the 12-bar blues progression.* "T for Texas," "I'm Movin' On," "Move It on Over," "Folsom Prison Blues," "Honky Tonk Blues" and "Muleskinner Blues" are a few examples. Here's a 12-bar blues in G:

Key of G

Each of the 12 bars (measures) in the above blues progression has 4 beats. The repeat sign (∕⁝) means play another bar of the chord in the previous bar.

The following flat-picked, chord-based solo is a 12-bar blues. It features many "blue notes" (flatted thirds, fifths and sevenths). Before you play it, here's how to add blue notes to the three chord fragments (the F, D and barre formations):

Ff. Blue Notes   **Df. Blue Notes**   **Barre Blue Notes**

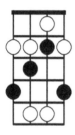 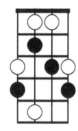 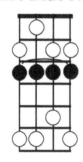

◯ = blue notes

Blue Note Boogie

SUMMING UP — NOW YOU KNOW...

▶ *How to locate three different chord families for any key*

▶ *How to use all three chord families to play licks and solos*

▶ *How to add "blue notes" to the chord fragments*

▶ The meaning of these musical terms:

I Chord, IV Chord, V Chord, Chord Family, 12-Bar Blues, Blue Notes, Hammer-on, Pull-off

THREE MOVEABLE MAJOR SCALES

G Major Scales

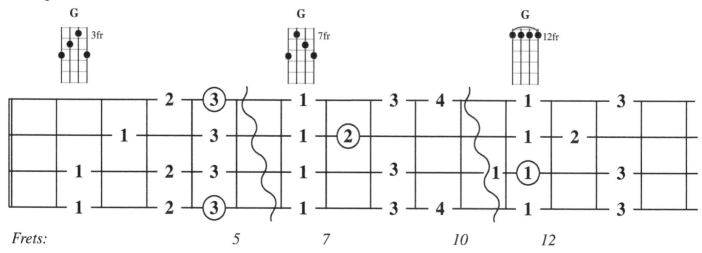

Frets: 5   7   10   12

WHY?

▶ The moveable major scales help you play melodies and ad lib solos in any key, all over the fretboard. They bring you a step closer to any player's goal: to be able to *play* whatever you can hear.

WHAT?

▶ *The numbers on the fretboard in* **ROADMAP #7** *are left-hand fingering suggestions.*

▶ *The three scales of* **ROADMAP #7** *are based on the three chord fragments* of **ROADMAPS #5** and **6**. The root notes (all G's in this diagram) are circled. Play the appropriate chord fragment to get your fretting hand "in position" to play one of the major scales. For example, play an F formation at the 3rd fret to play the lowest G scale of **ROADMAP #7**.

HOW?

▶ *Here are the three G scales that match the three G chord fragments.* Play the chord fragment before playing the scale. Start each scale with its root note so you can recognize the "do-re-mi" sound you have heard all your life!

Ff./G Scale

Df./G Major Scale

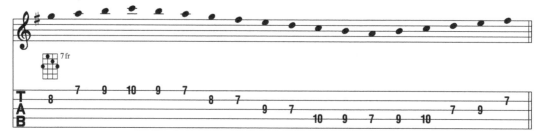

Barre/G Major Scale

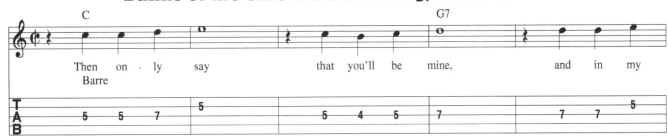

▶ *You can base a solo on the major scale that matches a song's key.* If a song is in the key of C, you can often ad lib C major scale licks throughout, even though the song has many chord changes.

DO IT!

▶ *Use major scales to play melodies.* For example, here's the basic melody to an old folk song, "Banks of the Ohio."

Banks of the Ohio (Basic Melody, Barre/C)

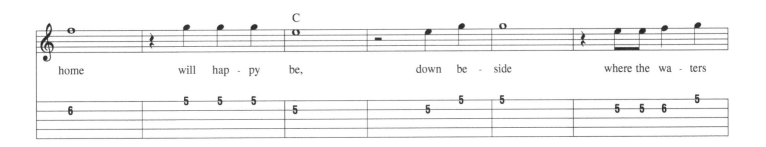

Then on - ly say that you'll be mine, and in my
Barre

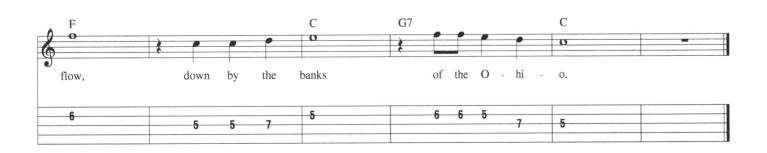

home will hap - py be, down be - side where the wa - ters

flow, down by the banks of the O - hi - o.

Fill out that basic melody, clawhammer style, or with bluegrass picking:

Banks of the Ohio (Bluegrass and Clawhammer Style)

You could also play "Banks of the Ohio" in the F position. Here's the basic melody:

Banks of the Ohio (Basic Melody Ff./Key of G)

Here's a three-finger picking arrangement based on the previous melody:

Banks of the Ohio (Bluegrass Style, Ff./Key of G)

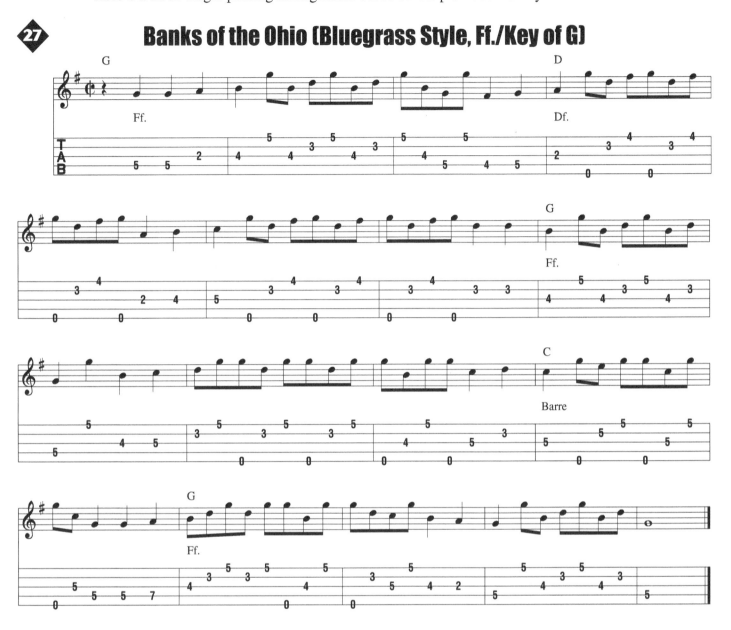

In the following arrangement of the old folk blues, "Corrine, Corinna," the melody is played with the D formation/F major scale, and embellished with the basic strum. (Tune your 5th string to A. Match it to the 1st string/7th fret.)

Corrine, Corinna (Df./Key of F)

▶ *Use major scales to jam.* The following solo to the old country tune, "Bury Me Beneath the Willow," makes use of two G major scale positions. In the first half of the tune, the melody is played with some ornamentation, using the barre formation/G major scale. During the second half, the soloist makes up a new melody based on the chord progression, using the F formation/G major scale.

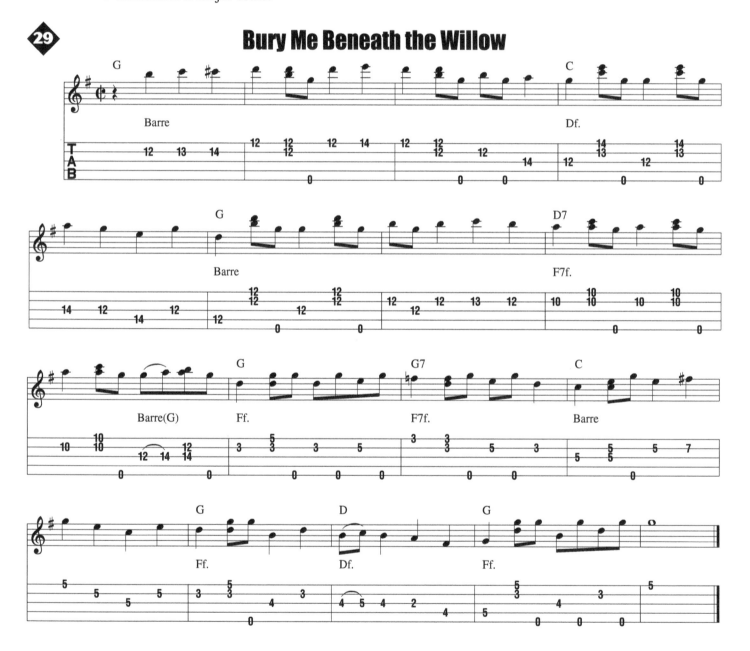

SUMMING UP — NOW YOU KNOW...

▶ *How to play three moveable major scales for each key*

▶ *How to use them to play melodies*

▶ *How to use them to ornament a melody and ad lib solos*

#8 MELODIC SCALES

G Major Positions

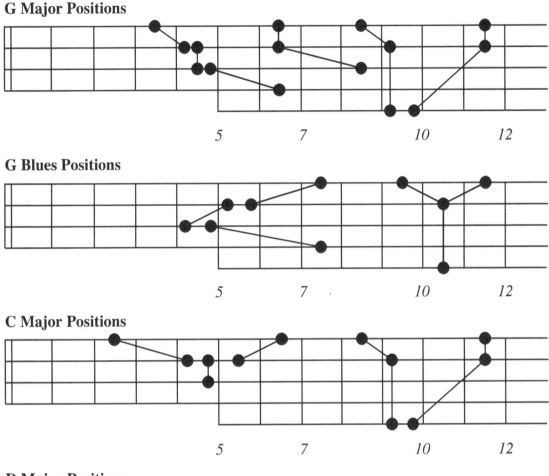

G Blues Positions

C Major Positions

D Major Positions

WHY?

▶ Using the fretboard positions of **ROADMAP #8**, you can play three-finger style major scale and blues scale licks that can't be played using Scruggs rolls. The melodic style of picking, developed by Bill Keith, Bobby Thompson and other innovative pickers in the early 1960s, allows you to play fiddle tunes, reels, rags and even classical pieces. It also opens up a new bag of improvisational tricks for bluegrassers.

WHAT?

▶ *Each of the fretboard positions allows you to play a whole set of melodic licks and phrases.*

▶ *Each of the fretboards of* **ROADMAP #8** *shows the positions that work well with a particular scale, such as G major or C major.*

► *You can use the "melodic positions" to play melodies, ornament melodies and to ad-lib licks or entire solos,* just as you did with major scales in **ROADMAPS #3** and **#7**.

► *Here are some sample melodic phrases and licks that can be played using the melodic positions of* **ROADMAP #8.**

▷ Some of the melodic scale positions include the fretted 5th string. Some people like to fret the 5th string with their thumb (reaching over the top of the neck); others prefer to fret the 5th string with a finger.

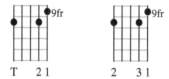

▷ A few of the melodic positions that are written over the tablature include spots in parenthesis. These are notes that you fret during *part of a lick.* For example, during the 5th *G Major Lick* that follows, the 1st string is fretted at the 9th fret, then at the 12th fret, then at the 9th fret again.

30

G Major Licks

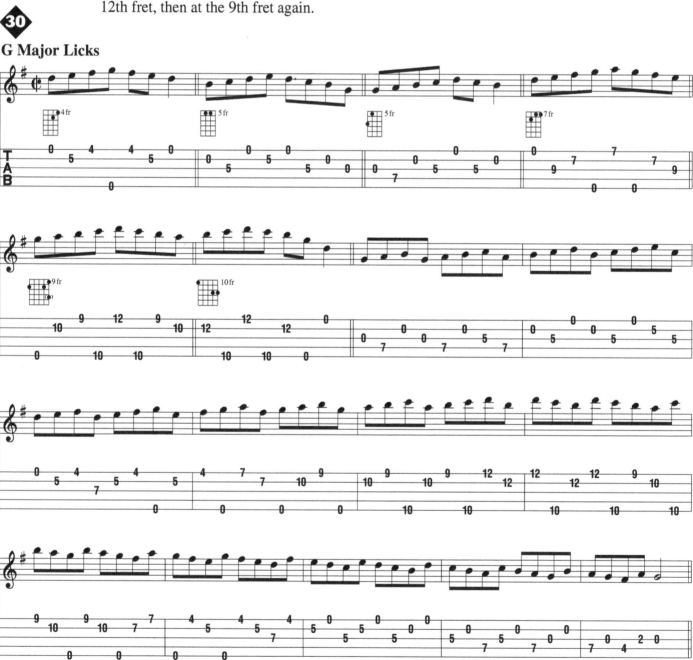

G Blues Licks

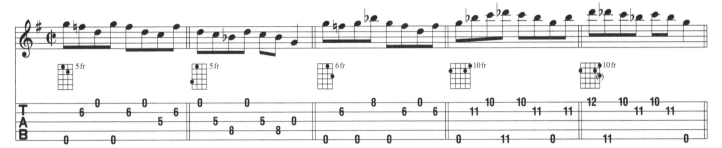

C Major Licks

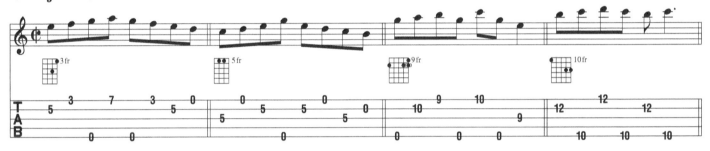

D Major Licks

HOW?

▶ *If a tune is in the key of G, you can ad lib solos using all the G major or G blues positions throughout.* But the blues scales should only be used when you want to impart a strong blues flavor to your solos.

▶ *Similarly, use C scale positions in the key of C.*

▶ *You can also change positions with a song's chord changes* (use a D scale on a D chord, a C scale on a C chord, etc.).

DO IT!

► In "Redwing," below, the soloist uses G major melodic scales to state and embellish the melody, much as a fiddler would. Notice how well melodic scales combine with Scruggs-style picking.

Redwing

► Here's the same song in the key of C, using C major melodic scales.

Redwing (In C)

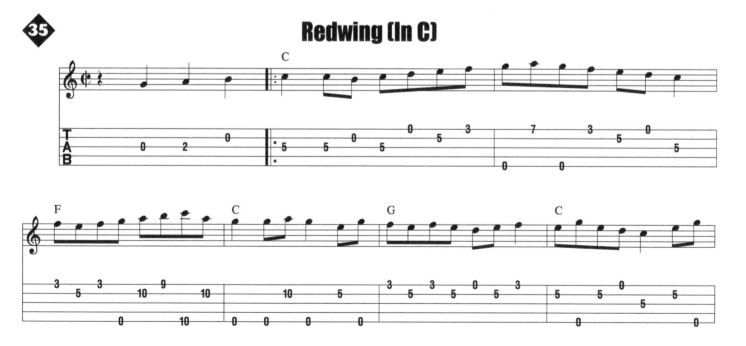

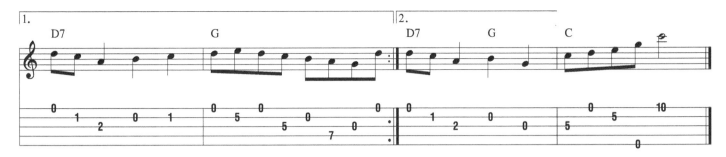

▶ Here's a melodic version of the first half of a popular fiddle tune, "The Eighth of January."
It shows how melodic scales can help a banjo player imitate fiddle licks.

The Eighth of January

▶ In the following tune, "Nine Pound Hammer," the first eight bars make use of G major
melodic scales, and the next eight bars of soloing are based on G blues melodic scales.
The solo occasionally alludes to the melody.

Nine Pound Hammer (With Melodic Licks)

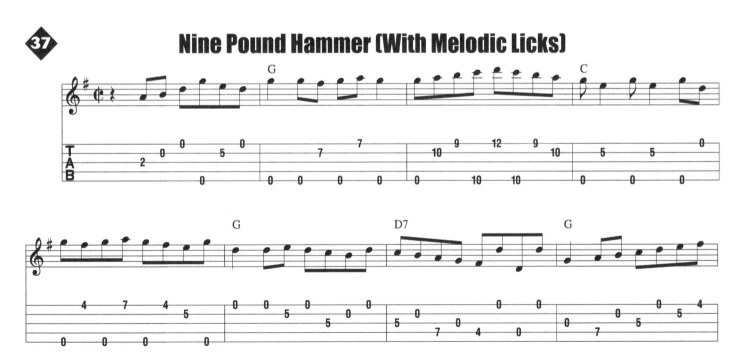

▶ Here's an ad lib solo to a tune with similar changes to "Sweet Georgia Brown." The soloist changes scales with the tune's chord changes. When you use this method, be aware that seventh chords (A7, D7, etc.) resolve "up a fourth" (A7 resolves to D, for example); for this reason *it often is appropriate to use a scale that is a fourth above the seventh chord*. For A7, you can use an A scale or a D scale; for D7, you can use a D scale or a G scale.

Whistling Wilt

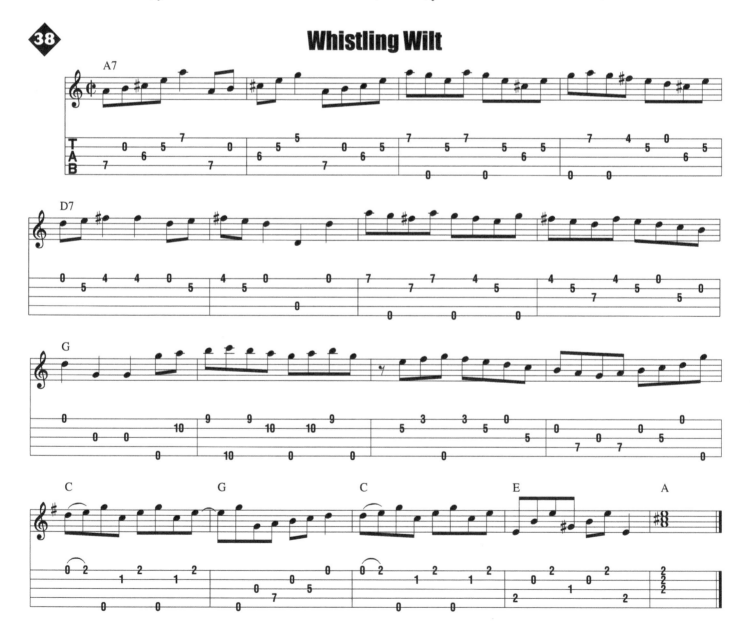

► This excerpt from Bach's "Jesu, Joy of Man's Desiring" shows how melodic scales can be used to play classical pieces.

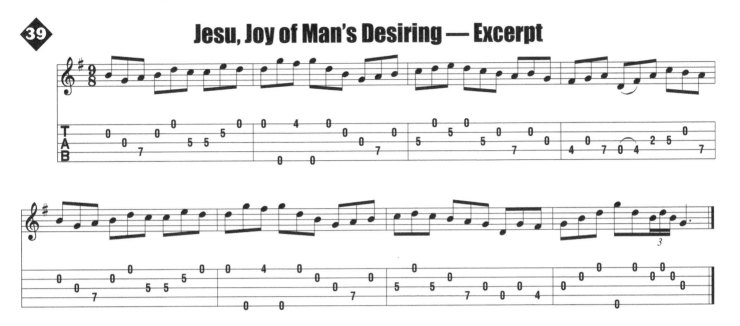

Jesu, Joy of Man's Desiring — Excerpt

SUMMING UP — NOW YOU KNOW...

► *How to play major and blues "melodic" scales in several keys, using many positions*

► *How to use these scales to play and ornament a melody*

► *How to improvise freely, using melodic scales, in G and C*

#9 THE CIRCLE-OF-FIFTHS

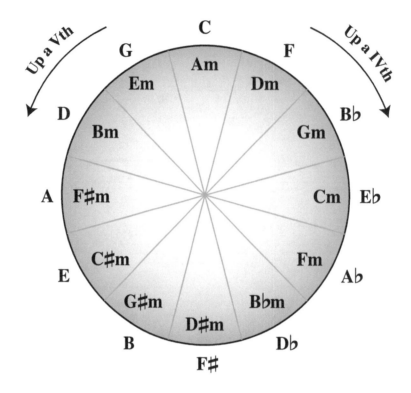

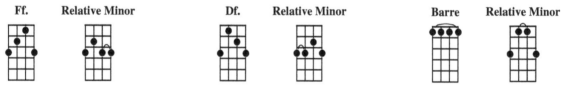

WHY?

▶ Many songs include more than just the I, IV and V chords. These subtler chord progressions are easier to understand and play once you are acquainted with relative minors and circle-of-fifths movement.

WHAT?

▶ The circle-of-fifths (also called the "circle-of-fourths") arranges the twelve musical notes so that *a step counter-clockwise takes you up a fifth, and a step clockwise takes you up a fourth.*

▷ Counter-clockwise: G is a fifth above C, B a fifth above E, etc.

▷ Clockwise: F is a fourth above C, B♭ is a fourth above F, etc.

▶ *Every major chord has a relative minor chord* that has many of the same notes as its relative major. The relative minor is the VI chord; A is the sixth note in the C major scale, so Am is the relative minor to a C major chord.

▶ *Am is relative minor to C; C is relative major to Am.*

▶ *If a song includes minor chords, they are usually the relative minors of the I, IV and V chords.*

► *The chord grids in* **ROADMAP #9** *show how to alter each of the three moveable major chords to play its relative minor:*

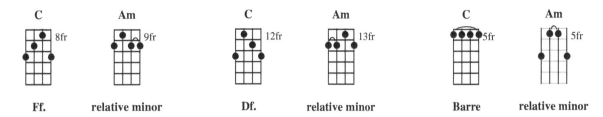

HOW?

► *In circle-of-fifths progressions, you leave the I chord (creating tension) and come back to I (resolving tension) by clockwise motion,* going up by fourths until you are "home" at the I chord. For example, in the following key-of-C progression, which resembles the bluegrass/blues standard "Salty Dog," you jump to the A7 chord (leaving the C chord family) and then get back to C by going clockwise along the circle: D7 is a fourth above A, G7 is a fourth above D7 and C is a fourth above G7. Strum the progression:

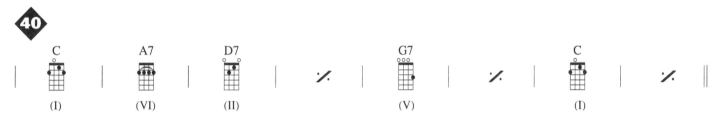

This is a I-VI-II-V progression, because A is a sixth above C, D is a fifth above C, and so on. In one variation of this sequence (as in "Don't Let Your Deal Go Down"), you start on the VI chord. For example, in the key of F:

► *As you move clockwise along the circle, the chords can be major or minor,* but the V chord is almost always a 7th.

► *If you use moveable chords, refer back to* **ROADMAP #6** *to remember how to move up a IVth:*

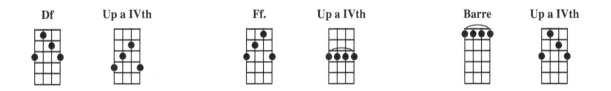

45

Here's a clawhammer version of a song with the "Don't Let Your Deal Go Down" progression, played with moveable chords:

Call Me a Dog

▶ This circle-of-fifths progression resembles "Alice's Restaurant," and many other tunes, including Robert Johnson's "They're Red Hot" and Bob Wills' "Bring It on Down to My House, Honey." In fact, every acoustic blues player, past and present, has a song with this progression. Strum four downstrokes per bar:

Raggy Blues

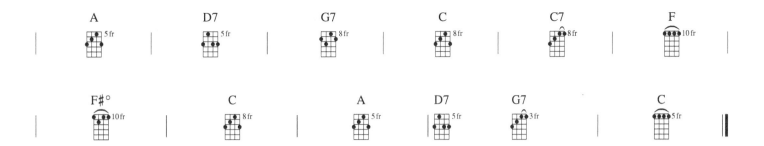

DO IT!

▶ *Play the I–vi–ii–V7 progression in many keys.* (The use of lower-case roman numerals indicates *minor chords.*) This progression is so common that pros have nicknamed it "standard changes," "ice cream changes," "I Got Rhythm" changes (after the Gershwin song), or just "the rhythm changes," for short. It's the basis for countless standards ("Blue Moon," "Heart and Soul,") and "classic rock" tunes ("Oh, Donna," "Stand by Me," "Every Time You Go Away," "Every Breath You Take").

44

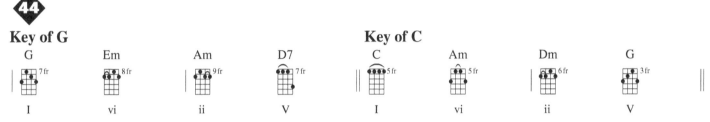

Sometimes the IV chord is played instead of the minor ii chord. It's a small change because the IV chord is the relative major of ii; in the key of C, for example, Dm is ii, and F, its relative major, is IV.

▶ *Play VII–III–VI–II–V–I progressions,* like "Mister Sandman" and "Red Roses for a Blue Lady." In these tunes, you jump halfway around the circle, from I (or C, in the key of C) to VII (B7); then you cycle back to C by going up a fourth (to E7), up another fourth (to A7) and so on, until you reach the C chord:

45
Key of C

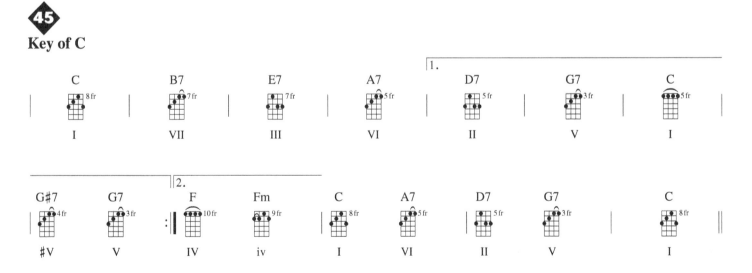

► *Play and analyze this old jazz standard,* which mostly consists of circle-of-fifths chord movement:

I Used to Love You (But It's All Over)

> ▷ The Roman numerals between the music and tablature are there to help you identify the chords in terms of intervals and understand chord movement.

> ▷ Notice how many times the chords move from I to VI and cycle back to I (VI–II–V–I).

> ▷ At one point, you cycle back from the III chord (A7), giving you a III–VI–II–V–I progression, one step farther on the circle than VI–II–V–I.

SUMMING UP — NOW YOU KNOW...

► *How to play circle-of-fifths progressions in any key, including "Rhythm Changes"*

► *How to automatically find the relative minor of any moveable major chord*

► *How to automatically find the chord that is a fourth above any moveable major chord*

► *The meaning of these musical terms:* Relative Minor, Relative Major, Rhythm Changes, Standard Changes

#10 USING THE CAPO

Open Strings = B♭

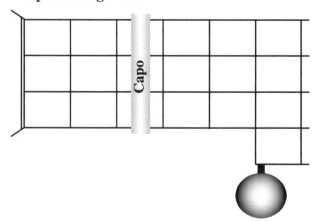

1st Position C Chord = D

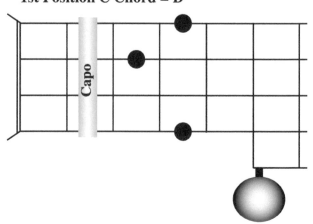

WHY?

▶ Bluegrass, old-time and folk banjo players often use a capo to play in keys other than G or C. This is because G and C are the easiest G tuning keys; and the capo makes it possible to play standard, popular G and C licks, and phrases in all keys.

▶ You can also use the capo to raise the pitch of an *arrangement.* Many popular fiddle tunes are in A and D, because those are the easiest keys for fiddle. Banjo players can play these tunes more easily in G or C; and the capo makes it possible to move G and C arrangements up to A and D, to match a fiddler.

WHAT?

▶ *Clamping a capo around the banjo neck raises the instrument's pitch.* If you capo at the first fret and play a first position G chord, it sounds like G♯. With the capo at the second fret, a first position G sounds like A.

▶ *Moveable chords are not affected by the capo.* If the capo is on the first fret (for playing in the key of G♯) a barre chord at the actual 5th fret is still a C. But a barre five frets above the capo is the IV chord (C♯).

HOW?

▶ *To move a banjo arrangement to a higher key, go forward in the alphabet and capo as many steps up the neck.*

▷ To move (transpose) your key-of-G arrangement of a fiddle tune to the key of A, capo on the second fret, because A is a whole step (two frets) above G.

▷ To transpose your key-of-C arrangement of a fiddle tune up to the key of D, capo at the second fret; D is a whole step above C.

▷ If you've learned a key-of-C arrangement of a song but your voice is more comfortable in E, capo at the 4th fret. E is two whole steps (four frets) above C.

▶ Usually, the use of a capo requires some 5th string adjustments. The chart on the next page shows how to retune the 5th string to match various keys and capo configurations. The general idea is to tune the 5th string to a note that is in the I chord of the key in which you're playing.

► *The following chart shows how to use the capo to play in any key.*

  ▷ Most bluegrass and old-time banjo players capo, as shown below, to play in the key of A, B♭ and B, so they can use standard key-of-G licks.

  ▷ Most jazz or Dixieland banjo players do not use a capo.

  ▷ In the **ROADMAP #3** chapter, you learned how to play in D, E and F with no capo. This chapter presents another way to play in those keys, using a capo.

To play in the key of…	capo at fret #	and play a 1st position	tune 5th string
A♭	1	G	A♭ (up 1 fret)
A	2	G	A (up 2 frets)
B♭	3	G	B♭ (up 3 frets)
B	4	G	B (up 4 frets)
C	5	G	C (up 5 frets)
or C	no capo	C	no change
D♭	1	C	A♭ (up 1 fret)
D	2	C	A (up 2 frets)
E♭	3	C	B♭ (up 3 frets)
E	4	C	B (up 4 frets)
F	5	C	C (up 5 frets)
G♭	6	C	D♭ (up 6 frets)
G	no capo	G	no change

DO IT!

► *Make sure you can use the capo to solve these problems:*

  ▷ You've learned to play the fiddle tune "Billy in the Low Ground" in G, but most fiddlers play it in C. Where do you put the capo to match them? (As the above chart shows, capo on the 5th fret and play your G arrangement.)

  ▷ A songbook has one of your favorite tunes written in the key of E♭. You can sing it in that key, but how can you use the capo to make it easier to play? (As the chart says, capo on the 3rd fret and play as if you were in the key of C. Where the book says "E♭," play a C. Similarly, all chords will be three frets lower than the ones in the book: for A♭, play F; for B♭7, play G7, and so on.)

▷ You're learning a song from an album. The artist sings it in the key of B♭, which is too low for your voice. What do you do? (You could play it in C, which is two frets higher than B♭, or D, which is 4 frets higher. For the key of C, no capo is needed; for the key of D, capo at the 2nd fret and play as you would in the key of C.)

▷ Another song on the same album is in F, and it's too *high* for your voice. What do you do? (D is three frets lower than F, and C is five frets lower. If D is right for your voice, you could play "in the key of C" with the capo at the 2nd fret; for the key of C, you need no capo.

SUMMING UP — NOW YOU KNOW...

▶ How to use a capo to play in any key, using first position chords

▶ How to use a capo to raise the key of a banjo arrangement

▶ How to use a capo to change a song's key to suit your voice

USING THE PRACTICE TRACKS

The **ROADMAPS** illuminate many soloing styles, including:

- ▶ *first position major scales*
- ▶ *moveable major chord licks*
- ▶ *moveable major scales*
- ▶ *melodic scales*

On the five practice tracks, the banjo is separated from the rest of the band—it's on one side of your stereo. You can tune it out and use the band as backup, trying out any soloing techniques you like. You can also imitate the banjo; here are the soloing ideas on each track:

 #1 Bury Me Beneath the Willow (In G, C, D, F and E)

This I–IV–I–V tune is played five times, in five different keys. The banjo uses the major scale of each key to play the melody, clawhammer style, with some embellishment. It starts in G, then modulates to C, D, F and E. The 5th string is tuned to A for the keys of D and F, and to B for the key of E.

 #2 Take This Hammer (In G)

The first time around, the soloist ad libs chord-based licks, bluegrass style, using moveable chords in the G chord family in which the I chord is a D formation. The second chorus is the same, but the chord family with a barred G/I chord is used. The third time, it's the chord family with an F formation/G chord. The fourth time, the soloist uses the **F-D-BARRE ROADMAP (#5)** to play many inversions of each chord; the solo is based on the resulting variations.

 #3 Worried Man Blues (In A)

The banjo is capoed at the 2nd fret, the 5th string tuned up to A, and the 12-bar tune is played three times. The first time, the bluegrass-style solo is based on the major scale of the D formation/A chord. The second time, the barred A chord's major scale is used, and the third time the F formation/A chord's major scale is the basis for the solo.

 #4 Wabash Cannonball (In G, C and D)

The first two solos employ many melodic licks in G, first using major scale positions, then using G blues positions. The third time around the 16-bar tune, the song modulates to C and the solo is based on key-of-C melodic licks. Then the song modulates to D, and the banjo plays key-of-D melodic licks.

 #5 Won't You Come Home Bill Bailey (In G and C)

In this classic Dixieland tune, the banjo strums the melody, with some ad lib embellishments, in the key of G. The second time around the 32-bar song, the banjo does the same in the key of C. The 5th string is almost completely unused.

LISTENING SUGGESTIONS

Recordings are available by all these great banjo players. Look for videos, also, and go see them perform, whenever possible!

BLUEGRASS

Some of the pioneers:

Earl Scruggs (listen to the early Flatt and Scruggs recordings)
Ralph Stanley (his own recordings and those of the Stanley Brothers)
Don Reno (especially Reno and Smiley recordings)
Bill Monroe (the father of bluegrass always had a good banjo player in his band, and the old recordings from the late 1940s that included Flatt and Scruggs are like the Rosetta Stone of bluegrass)
Doug Dillard (with the Dillards)
Allen Shelton (with early Jim and Jesse McReynolds recordings)
Sonny Osborne (with the Osborne Brothers)

Some major players from the second and third generations:

Bill Keith
Eddie Adcock
John Hartford
Tony Trischka
Pete Wernick
Bela Fleck
Tony Furtado

The video *High Lonesome* is a good introduction to bluegrass music, and so is the CD *Will the Circle Be Unbroken*. The movie *O Brother, Where Art Thou* also features old-time and bluegrass music.

TRADITIONAL (CLAWHAMMER AND TWO-FINGER PICKING)

Bascom Lamar Lunsford
Grandpa Jones
Uncle Dave Macon
Charlie Poole
Roscoe Holcomb
Clarence Ashley
Ola Belle Reed
Buell Kazee
Mark Schatz
Tommy Jarrell
Wade Ward
Fred Cockerham

DIXIELAND/JAZZ BANJO

Most Dixieland or jazz banjoists play 4-string (tenor or plectrum) banjos. Listen to these legendary pickers and try to imitate them on 5-string:

Roy Smeck
Eddie Peabody
Harry Reser
Smokey Montgomery (with the Light Crust Doughboys, the Western swing band)

ABOUT THE AUTHOR

Fred Sokolow is a versatile "musicians' musician." Besides fronting his own jazz, bluegrass and rock bands, Fred has toured with Bobbie Gentry, Jim Stafford, Tom Paxton, Ian Whitcomb, Jody Stecher and The Limeliters, playing guitar, banjo, mandolin and Dobro. His music has been heard on many TV shows (*Survivor, Dr. Quinn*), commercials, and movies.

Sokolow has written nearly a hundred stringed instrument books and videos for seven major publishers. This library of instructional material, which teaches jazz, rock, bluegrass, country and blues guitar, banjo, Dobro and mandolin, is sold on six continents. He also teaches musical seminars on the West Coast. A jazz CD, two rock guitar and two banjo recordings, which showcase Sokolow's technique, all received excellent reviews in the U.S. and Europe.

If you think Sokolow still isn't versatile enough, know that he MC'd for Carol Doda at San Francisco's legendary Condor Club, accompanied a Russian balalaika virtuoso at the swank Bonaventure Hotel in L.A., won the *Gong Show,* played lap steel and banjo on the *Tonight Show,* picked Dobro with Chubby Checker, played mandolin with Rick James and wrote and performed the music score for the movie *Rampaging Nurses*!

GREAT BANJO PUBLICATIONS

FROM HAL LEONARD

Hal Leonard Banjo Method
by Mac Robertson, Robbie Clement, Will Schmid
This innovative method teaches 5-string banjo bluegrass style using a carefully paced approach that keeps beginners playing great songs *while learning*. Book 1 covers easy chord strums, tablature, right-hand rolls, hammer-ons, slides and pull-offs, and more. Book 2 includes solos and licks, fiddle tunes, back-up, capo use, and more.

00699500 Book 1 Book Only $9.99
00695101 Book 1 Book/Online Audio $17.99
00699502 Book 2 Book Only $9.99

Banjo Chord Finder
00695741 9 x 12......................................$8.99
00695742 6 x 9......................................$7.99

Banjo Scale Finder
00695783 6 x 9......................................$6.99

Banjo Aerobics
A 50-Week Workout Program for Developing, Improving and Maintaining Banjo Technique
by Michael Bremer
Take your banjo playing to the next level with this fantastic daily resource, providing a year's worth of practice material with a two-week vacation. The accompanying audio includes demo tracks for all the examples in the book to reinforce how the banjo should sound.

00113734 Book/Online Audio $22.99

Earl Scruggs and the 5-String Banjo
Earl Scruggs' legendary method has helped thousands of banjo players get their start. It features everything you need to know to start playing, even how to build your own banjo! Topics covered include: Scruggs tuners • how to read music • chords • how to read tablature • anatomy of Scruggs-style picking • exercises in picking • 44 songs • biographical notes • and more! The online audio features Earl Scruggs playing and explaining over 60 examples!

00695764 Book Only......................................$29.99
00695765 Book/Online Audio $39.99

First 50 Songs You Should Play on Banjo
arr. Michael J. Miles & Greg Cahill
Easy-to-read banjo tab, chord symbols and lyrics for the most popular songs banjo players like to play. Explore clawhammer and three-finger-style banjo in a variety of tunings and capoings with this one-of-a-kind collection. Songs include: Angel from Montgomery • Carolina in My Mind • Cripple Creek • Danny Boy • The House of the Rising Sun • Mr. Tambourine Man • Take Me Home, Country Roads • This Land Is Your Land • Wildwood Flower • and many more.
00153311 ....$15.99

Fretboard Roadmaps
by Fred Sokolow
This handy book/with online audio will get you playing all over the banjo fretboard in any key! You'll learn to: increase your chord, scale and lick vocabulary • play chord-based licks, moveable major and blues scales, melodic scales and first-position major scales • and much more! The audio includes 51 demonstrations of the exercises.

00695358 Book/Online Audio $17.99

The Great American Banjo Songbook
70 Songs
arr. Alan Munde & Beth Mead-Sullivan
Explore the repertoire of the "Great American Songbook" with this 70-song collection, masterfully arranged by Alan Munde and Beth Mead-Sullivan for 3-finger, Scruggs-style 5-string banjo. Rhythm tab, right hand fingerings and chord diagrams are included for each of these beloved melodies. Songs include: Ain't She Sweet • Blue Skies • Cheek to Cheek • Home on the Range • Honeysuckle Rose • It Had to Be You • Little Rock Getaway • Over the Rainbow • Sweet Georgia Brown • and more.
00156862 ....$19.99

How to Play the 5-String Banjo
Third Edition
by Pete Seeger
This basic manual for banjo players includes melody line, lyrics and banjo accompaniment and solos notated in standard form and tablature. Chapters cover material such as: a basic strum, the fifth string, hammering on, pulling off, double thumbing, and much more.

14015486 ....$19.99

O Brother, Where Art Thou?
Banjo tab arrangements of 12 bluegrass/folk songs from this Grammy-winning album. Includes: The Big Rock Candy Mountain • Down to the River to Pray • I Am a Man of Constant Sorrow • I Am Weary (Let Me Rest) • I'll Fly Away • In the Jailhouse Now • Keep on the Sunny Side • You Are My Sunshine • and more, plus lyrics and a banjo notation legend.

00699528 Banjo Tablature $17.99

Clawhammer Cookbook
Tools, Techniques & Recipes for Playing Clawhammer Banjo
by Michael Bremer
The goal of this book isn't to tell you how to play tunes or how to play like anyone else. It's to teach you ways to approach, arrange, and personalize any tune – to develop your own unique style. To that end, we'll take in a healthy serving of old-time music and also expand the clawhammer palate to taste a few other musical styles. Includes audio track demos of all the songs and examples to aid in the learning process.
00118354 Book/Online Audio $22.99

The Ultimate Banjo Songbook
A great collection of banjo classics: Alabama Jubilee • Bye Bye Love • Duelin' Banjos • The Entertainer • Foggy Mountain Breakdown • Great Balls of Fire • Lady of Spain • Orange Blossom Special • (Ghost) Riders in the Sky • Rocky Top • San Antonio Rose • Tennessee Waltz • UFO-TOFU • You Are My Sunshine • and more.

00699565 Book/Online Audio $29.99

Visit Hal Leonard online at **www.halleonard.com**

Prices, contents, and availability subject to change without notice.